Jake and THE BIG MACHINE

NICK WEBER

WestBow Press books may be ordered through booksellers or by contacting:

WestBow Press
A Division of Thomas Nelson & Zondervan
1663 Liberty Drive
Bloomington, IN 47403
www.westbowpress.com
844-714-3454

ISBN: 978-1-6642-4062-9 (sc)
ISBN: 978-1-6642-4063-6 (e)

Library of Congress Control Number: 2021914453

Print information available on the last page.

WestBow Press rev. date: 08/30/2021

WESTBOW
PRESS®
A DIVISION OF THOMAS NELSON
& ZONDERVAN

Jake and THE BIG MACHINE

Jake's eyes got big, wide and round.
His mouth dropped open, and he said
in a tiny, awed voice, "WOW."

"Stop Auntie, stop, stop, stop!"
Jake had spotted another construction
site and all the big machines were
running all over the place. "We have
to stop and watch," he cried.

It was always this way. Jake couldn't bear to pass by any big construction equipment without stopping to watch and study each machine. He was just amazed by how big and powerful the machines were and how much work they did. He could just watch them all day.

It didn't take him too long before he was learning the names of all the different machines. He learned about the cranes, the excavators, the backhoes, the mighty bulldozers and the front loaders.

There was only one thing he didn't like about the big machines and that was the very loud noise they all made because of the huge diesel engines that made them run.

As the weather got colder, Jake became sad when he couldn't see as many of the big machines working because all the construction work slowed down in the winter time.

Then one day he woke up and
it was Christmas morning! When
he went into the living room, his
Mommy said to him, "Jake, I think
Santa left something for you out in the garage."

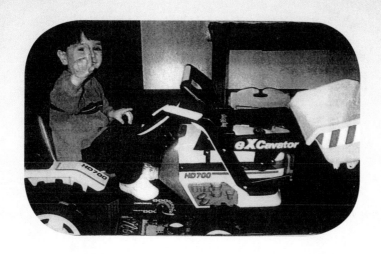

When he ran out there, there it was!
A big toy Front Loader! This one had
pedals, so Jake could drive it around
without all the noise of a big diesel
engine! Jake was just as happy as
he could be to have his
Very Own BIG MACHINE!

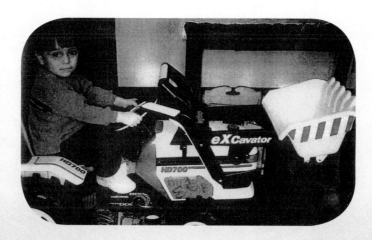

JaKe anD THe GIanT exCaVaTor

Jake just LOVED to watch
big construction equipment.

By the time he was two years old,
he could say the words
EX CA VA TOR and
STA BIL I ZOR.

He loved to watch them at work.
He loved them all, the BACKHOE, the
FRONT LOADER, the CRANE, and the
MIGHTY BULLDOZER. But his
favorite of all was the
EXCAVATOR!

One day he was walking past a construction site with his Auntie and they stopped to watch. There was a GIANT EXCAVATOR, with a bucket big enough for Jake to stand up in!

They were safely out of the way, but the man who was operating the GIANT EXCAVATOR, got out and walked over to them. "Hi, I'm Rich, what's your name?" Jake answered and said "My name is Jake". "I have a little boy at home just his size," Rich said to Auntie. "Would it be all right if he sat on my lap while I run the excavator?" "Oh boy, Auntie could I?" asked Jake. "Well, I guess it would be okay as long as you are very careful and do exactly what Rich says."

So Jake sat on Rich's lap and they scooped up dirt
with the front loader and put it in a pile.

Then they dug a hole with the backhoe and piled up the dirt so they could scoop it up with the front loader later.

Then they scooped up the dirt and
dumped it into a dump truck.

And that was the day that Jake got to
operate the GIANT EXCAVATOR!

Printed in the United States
by Baker & Taylor Publisher Services